Let's Roll
MONSTER TRUCKS

by Candice Ransom

FOCUS
READERS

www.northstareditions.com

Produced for North Star Editions by Red Line Editorial.

Photographs ©: Mikhail Kusayev/Dreamstime, cover, 1, 29; Barry Salmons/Shutterstock Images, 4–5, 20–21; Piotr Zajac/Shutterstock Images, 6; Malcolm Clarke/AP Images, 8–9; Maksim Shmeljov/Shutterstock Images, 11, 19; Michael Stokes/Shutterstock Images, 13; Natursports/Shutterstock Images, 14–15, 23; Marcel Jancovic/Shutterstock Images, 17; Juan Camilo Bernal/Shutterstock Images, 25; Pavel L Photo and Video/Shutterstock Images, 26–27

ISBN
978-1-63517-047-4 (hardcover)
978-1-63517-103-7 (paperback)
978-1-63517-204-1 (ebook pdf)
978-1-63517-154-9 (hosted ebook)

Library of Congress Control Number: 2016951022

Printed in the United States of America
Mankato, MN
November, 2016

About the Author

Candice Ransom used to ride on her stepfather's tractor. She loved trips in their green pickup, and she thinks old cars are the best. When she isn't writing books for children, she is driving on the back roads of Virginia in her own little red truck.

TABLE OF CONTENTS

CHAPTER 1

FLYING TRUCKS

Two monster trucks line up to race. Engines roar as the drivers steer around old cars. One truck drives right over the cars. The other truck gets stuck and loses.

 Monster trucks jump over rows of old cars.

Many monster trucks are named after popular characters.

Now it's time for the **freestyle** event. Each truck has 90 seconds to perform stunts. A monster truck crushes a row of cars like bugs. Then the truck stands up on its

two back tires. Now the truck slams
down on four wheels. It speeds
toward the smashed cars. The truck
hits the dirt ramp and soars over all
the cars.

People in the arena leap to
their feet. Monster trucks are fun
to watch!

FUN FACT

Monster trucks run best on special
clay-based dirt. Some tracks need 300
truckloads of dirt to fill an arena.

CHAPTER 2

BIGFOOT

In 1974, Bob Chandler bought a pickup truck. He tested his **four-wheel-drive** truck on hills. He added bigger tires and a stronger engine. Then he put 48-inch (122-cm) tires on his truck.

 Bigfoot was the best-known monster truck of the 1980s.

Chandler called his truck Bigfoot. He took the truck to auto shows and fairs. Bigfoot became famous.

Chandler decided to drive Bigfoot over two old cars in a cornfield. The truck crushed the cars like soda cans.

FUN FACT

Around 1980, promoter Bob George called Bigfoot a "monster truck," and the name stuck.

 Each tire on a monster truck weighs more than 800 pounds (363 kg).

Later, Chandler built Bigfoot 2. This truck had 66-inch (168-cm) tires that were taken from farm equipment. When Bigfoot 2 smashed cars, people went wild.

Other people began building their own giant-size trucks. They raced them and crushed cars. A new sport was born.

Chandler worried that the trucks were not safe. He helped form the

BIGFOOT

Bob Chandler found tires that were 10 feet (3.0 m) tall from a special Army truck used in Alaska. In 1986, Chandler built a truck to fit the enormous tires. Bigfoot 5 is 15 feet (4.6 m) tall, 13 feet (4.0 m) wide, and weighs 28,000 pounds (12,700 kg).

 Today's monster trucks are much safer than the monster trucks of the 1980s.

Monster Truck Racing Association. Guidelines controlled the size and weight of the trucks. Safety rules protected the drivers and the fans.

CHAPTER 3

MONSTER TRUCK BASICS

Monster trucks may look like regular trucks with giant tires, but they are very different. The **fiberglass** body can be molded into wild shapes. The frame is made of extra-strong steel tubing.

 Fans love to get up close to the monster trucks.

The driver sits in the center of the vehicle. The engine is mounted behind the seat to balance the truck's weight.

Monster trucks do not use regular gasoline. They use **methanol** for fuel. This fuel gives the engines more power.

FUN FACT

Monster trucks travel to events in haulers. The trucks' huge tires are replaced with smaller tires. That way, the trucks can fit inside the haulers.

PARTS OF A MONSTER TRUCK

driver's seat

engine

body

tires

The driver controls the front
wheels with the steering wheel.
A switch turns the rear wheels left
or right.

Monster trucks stand approximately 11 feet (3.4 m) tall and 12 feet (3.7 m) wide. Monster trucks weigh more than 10,000 pounds (4,536 kg). That's as much as an elephant weighs!

MONSTER TIRES

Monster trucks are great climbers. Their tires are 66 inches (168 cm) tall and 43 inches (109 cm) wide. The tire **treads** are cut down to reduce weight. Farm machinery tires work best because they are flexible. Earthmoving equipment tires are too stiff.

 **A monster truck burns 2.5 gallons (9.5 L) of fuel to drive 250 feet (76 m).**

CHAPTER 4

BUILDING BETTER MONSTER TRUCKS

Monster trucks bash into one another and crunch over objects. The trucks are designed to be tough, fast, and safe. Designers use computers to create frames that are both light and strong.

Monster trucks are designed to keep drivers as safe as possible.

A roll cage is built inside the frame. The roll cage keeps the driver safe if the truck rolls over. Heavy **axles** can take high jumps without snapping.

COMPUTER-AIDED DESIGN

Computer-aided design (CAD) software programs help architects and engineers design many products, including houses and cars. People draw on a digital tablet with a special pen. They can see their design in three dimensions. Lightweight monster truck frames are created with CAD.

 Monster truck frames can be many different shapes and colors.

Drivers wear **fire-resistant** suits, gloves, and shoes. They must wear helmets and safety harnesses.

Kill switches stop runaway trucks. These switches turn off the engine's power if the truck is out of control. One switch is next to the steering wheel. A second switch is on the back of the truck. A third switch is on a remote-controlled radio carried by a track official.

FUN FACT

In 2013, Joe Sylvester set a record. He jumped a distance of 237.5 feet (72.4 m) in his truck, Bad Habit.

▷ **Fans pack the arena to watch monster trucks in action.**

Fans love monster trucks. Thanks to technology, these trucks are safer for everyone.

THE POWER OF TRIANGLES

A triangle has three sides. If pressure is put on any one point, the triangle keeps its shape. Engineers discovered that a monster truck frame made with triangles was stronger than a rectangular frame. Hollow tubes could be used instead of solid steel. Lighter materials made the truck lighter. The triangle-based frame is also safer.

Monster trucks are so heavy that they would bend rectangle-shaped frames.

FOCUS ON
MONSTER TRUCKS

Write your answers on a separate piece of paper.

1. Write a sentence that describes the key ideas from Chapter 4.

2. Would you prefer to watch a monster truck race or a freestyle event? Why?

3. What turns a monster truck's rear wheels?
  A. an axle
  B. a switch
  C. a steering wheel

4. How would monster trucks be different without computer-aided design?
  A. They would have smaller tires.
  B. They would use a different fuel.
  C. They would be heavier and weaker.

5. What does **guidelines** mean in this book?

    A. people who drive

    B. sizes and weights of objects

    C. rules that people follow

Guidelines controlled the size and weight of the trucks. Safety rules protected the drivers and the fans.

6. What does **runaway** mean in this book?

    A. out of control

    B. switched off

    C. powerful

Kill switches stop **runaway** trucks. These switches turn off the engine's power if the truck is out of control.

Answer key on page 32.

GLOSSARY

axles
Bars on which wheels revolve.

fiberglass
A lightweight material made of tiny strands of glass combined to create a durable surface.

fire-resistant
Designed to resist burning and heat.

four-wheel-drive
Having a feature that allows all four of a vehicle's wheels to get power from the engine.

freestyle
An event in which the driver does tricks and stunts.

kill switches
Buttons or switches that shut off electrical power to an engine.

methanol
A colorless fuel made from alcohol.

treads
The parts of a tire that touch the ground.

TO LEARN MORE

BOOKS

Monnig, Alex. *Behind the Wheel of a Monster Truck*. Mankato, MN: The Child's World, 2016.

O'Hearn, Michael. *The Kids' Guide to Monster Trucks*. Mankato, MN: Capstone Press, 2010.

Savage, Jeff. *Monster Trucks*. Mankato, MN: Capstone Press, 2010.

NOTE TO EDUCATORS

Visit **www.focusreaders.com** to find lesson plans, activities, links, and other resources related to this title.

INDEX

Answer Key: 1. Answers will vary; **2.** Answers will vary; **3.** B; **4.** C; **5.** C; **6.** A

DATE DUE

			PRINTED IN U.S.A.